DATE DUE

20			

Super Senses

Smelling

Mary Mackill

Heinemann Library
Chicago, Illinois

© 2006 Heinemann Library
a division of Reed Elsevier Inc.
Chicago, Illinois

Customer Service 888-454-2279

Visit our website at www.heinemannraintree.com

Printed and bound in China by South China Printing Company Limited
Photo research by Hannah Taylor and Fiona Orbell
Designed by Jo Hinton-Malivoire and bigtop

10 09 08 07 06
10 9 8 7 6 5 4 3 2 1

Library of Congress Cataloging-in-Publication Data
Mackill, Mary.
  Smelling / Mary Mackill.
      p. cm. -- (Super senses)
  Includes bibliographical references and index.
  ISBN 1-4034-7377-3 (library binding-hardcover : alk. paper) -- ISBN 1-4034-7384-6 (pbk. : alk. paper)
  1. Smell--Juvenile literature. I. Title. II. Series: Mackill, Mary. Super senses.
  QP458.M33 2006
  612.8'6--dc22

                                        2005018944

Acknowledgments
The publishers would like to thank the following for permission to reproduce photographs:
Alamy Images pp. **13** (BananaStock), **17** (David Hoffman Photo Library), **4** (South West Images Scotland); Bubbles p. **9** (Loisjoy Thurstun); Corbis pp. **10** (Bob Krist), **19** (Tom Brakefield); Getty Images pp. **18**, **23b** (AFP), **14**, **23a** (Botanica), **12** (FoodPix), **5**, **7**, **23c** (Photodisc), **15**, **22** (Photographer's Choice), **16** (Taxi), **6** (The Image Bank); Harcourt Education Ltd pp. **20**, **21** (Tudor Photography); Science Photo Library p. **11** (Astrid & Hanns-Frieder Michler).

Cover photograph reproduced with permission of Getty Images/DK Stock.

Every effort has been made to contact copyright holders of any material reproduced in this book. Any omissions will be rectified in subsequent printings if notice is given to the publisher.

Many thanks to the teachers, library media specialists, reading instructors, and educational consultants who have helped develop the Read and Learn/Lee y aprende brand.

Disclaimer
All the Internet addresses (URLs) given in this book were valid at the time of going to press. However, due to the dynamic nature of the Internet, some addresses may have changed, or sites may have changed or ceased to exist since publication. While the author and publishers regret any inconvenience this may cause readers, no responsibility for any such changes can be accepted by either the author or the publishers.

The paper used to print this book comes from sustainable resources.

Contents

Some words are shown in bold, **like this**. You can find out what they mean by looking in the glossary.

What Are My Senses?

You have five **senses**. They help you see, hear, taste, smell, and touch things.

Pretend you are in a garden.

What can you smell?

Smelling is one of your five senses.

What Do I Use to Smell?

Most things give off a smell.

This is called a **scent**.

Your nose picks up these scents.

Your nose learns what different things smell like.

How Does My Sense of Smell Work?

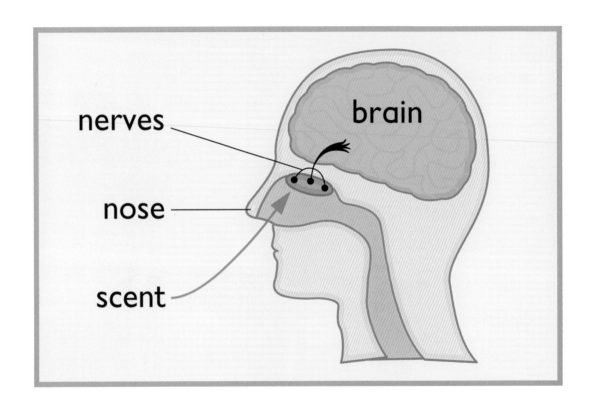

Smells come in to your nose and hit **nerves**.

The nerves send a message to your brain.

Your brain picks up the message.

Your brain would tell you that
this sock smells bad!

What Can I Smell?

Trees and flowers have different **scents**.

Food that has gone bad can
have a strong, bad smell.

How Does My Sense of Smell Help Me?

Your **sense** of smell helps you stay safe.

Smelling smoke could mean that something is on fire.

The smell of food can make you feel hungry!

How Can I Smell Things Better?

Try to **breathe** in deeply.

More smells will come in through your nose.

Put your nose close to something.
You can smell it better.

How Can I Take Care of My Sense of Smell?

Try to stay healthy.

It is harder to smell if you have a cold.

Be careful not to **breathe** in
dangerous smells.

Animals Have a Sense of Smell, Too!

Some animals have a very good **sense** of smell.

Dogs can find people by smelling their **scent**.

A skunk sprays a bad scent to keep other animals away!

Test Your Sense of Smell

Hold your nose and eat a piece of chocolate.

Drink some water.

Stop holding your nose and eat another piece of chocolate.

Which piece of chocolate could
you taste better?

Smelling food helps you taste
it better.

Smelling Is Super!

Your **sense** of smell:

- tells you if food has gone bad

- warns you if something is on fire

- lets you know when tasty food is ready to eat!

Glossary

 breathe taking in air into your body. You can smell things by breathing in through your nose.

 **nerve** part inside your body. Nerves work with the brain to sense things.

 **scent** smell that is given off by something

 **sense** something that helps you see, touch, taste, smell, and hear the things around you

Index

Note to Parents and Teachers

Reading for information is an important part of a child's literacy development. Learning begins with a question about something. Help children think of themselves as investigators and researchers by encouraging their questions about the world around them. Each chapter in this book begins with a question. Read the question together. Look at the pictures. Talk about what you think the answer might be. Then read the text to find out if your predictions were correct. Think of other questions you could ask about the topic, and discuss where you might find the answers. Assist children in using the picture glossary and the index to practice new vocabulary and research skills.